DEAR GHOST,

ALSO BY CATHERINE OWEN

Somatic: The Life and Work of Egon Schiele
(Exile Editions, 1998)

The Wrecks of Eden
(Wolsak & Wynn, 2001)

Shall: ghazals
(Wolsak & Wynn, 2006)

Cusp/detritus: an experiment in alleyways
(Anvil Press, 2006)

DOG: sonnets
(with Joe Rosenblatt, Mansfield Press, 2008)

Frenzy
(Anvil Press, 2009)

Seeing Lessons
(Wolsak & Wynn, 2010)

Trobairitz
(Anvil Press, 2012)

Catalysts: Confrontations with the Muse
(Wolsak & Wynn, 2012)

Designated Mourner
(ECW, 2014)

The Other 23 & a Half Hours: Or Everything You Wanted to Know that Your MFA Didn't Teach You
(Wolsak & Wynn, 2015)

The Day of the Dead: Sliver Fictions, Short Stories & an Homage
(Caitlin Press, 2016)

DEAR GHOST,

CATHERINE OWEN
POEMS

A Buckrider Book

© Catherine Owen, 2017

No part of this publication may be reproduced, stored in a retrieval system or transmitted, in any form or by any means, without the prior written consent of the publisher or a license from the Canadian Copyright Licensing Agency (Access Copyright). For an Access Copyright license, visit www.accesscopyright.ca or call toll free to 1-800-893-5777.

Buckrider Books is an imprint of Wolsak and Wynn Publishers.

Cover and interior design: Natalie Olsen, Kisscut Design
Cover image © Ruth Berkowitz / shutterstock.com
Author photograph: Bruce Meyer
Typeset in Ashbury
Printed by Coach House Printing Company Toronto, Canada

Canada Council for the Arts   Conseil des Arts du Canada

Canadian Heritage   Patrimoine canadien

ONTARIO ARTS COUNCIL
CONSEIL DES ARTS DE L'ONTARIO
an Ontario government agency
un organisme du gouvernement de l'Ontario

The publisher gratefully acknowledges the support of the Canada Council for the Arts, the Ontario Arts Council and the Canada Book Fund.

Buckrider Books
280 James Street North
Hamilton, ON
Canada L8R 2L3

Library and Archives Canada Cataloguing in Publication

Owen, Catherine
[Poems. Selections]
Dear ghost / Catherine Owen.

Poems.
ISBN 978-1-928088-31-8 (softcover)

I. Title.

PS8579.W43D43 2017   C811'.54   C2017-900983-4

*To my family, the film industry and John Ashbery;
and with deep thanks always to Wolsak & Wynn/Buckrider,
although they may eschew the random ampersand.*

DEAR GHOST, WHAT SHELTER IN THE NOONDAY CROWD?

JOHN ASHBERY, *"Light Turnouts"*

CONTENTS

13   A Prelude

POEMS THAT WERE OVERHEARD IN VARIOUS LOCALES

17   Decoupage
18   The Dildo Craftsman
19   Three Overheard Sonnets
22   Residual Lingerie
23   Thirled
25   Bible Study Group at the Beach
26   A Little Note on Passing By
27   Ocean, A Personal Ad
28   Just the Way Things Are (He Said)

POEMS THAT WORK IN THE TV WORLD

31   Movie Industry Trash
32   Shooting Afghanistan in Minaty Bay
33   The Stash
34   These are the Conditions
35   Two a.m., After Taking Hours to Shoot the Final Scene, North Van Memorial Grounds
36   Just Another Day in Film
37   The Deceased BGs
38   Cast Driver for Number One
39   When I Love Film the Most

POEMS THAT ATTEND TO FAMILIAR CHARACTERS FROM THE PAST

43	Washing
45	The Window Washer
47	Jigger
51	Steve Kulash, Taxidermist
52	Just Another Character in the Song of Songs
53	The Journal of John Berryman from 1948 to 1971: A reverse glosa of first lines
55	What I Remember about Attending Elementary School
56	What I Remember about Being Born
57	What I Remember about What We Weren't Allowed in Childhood
58	Nine: An Extended, Shortened Corona
67	Swallows' Nests of Isla de Janitzio, Michoacán
68	Just Another Loss of Faith
69	The Combination
70	My Parents are Playing Scrabble on the Deck
71	Against Billy Collins' Refusal to Read Poems called "My Grandfather's Binoculars"
72	Problems with the Sentimental Perspective Over a Construction Site and a Nazareth Concert, circa 2013
73	Two Stanzas on My Father Begun by Sharon Olds
74	This is a Picture of My Father Right after I was Born

POEMS THAT VEER INTO THE FREAKISH AND MAY ECHO JOHN ASHBERY

- 77 The Confidante of Bruised Fruit and Other Rides on the Subway
- 78 2:22 a.m.
- 79 Later on in January, Following the Century's Grand Upheaval
- 80 Hooks and Pulleys Galore
- 81 A Few Delightful Sound Bites from a Downtown Tragedy in Three Parts
- 82 Elegy with the Ghost of Larry Levis in It
- 85 The Social Net as Sturm Und Drang
- 86 Transformations in the Aviary of the Banal
- 87 Excerpts from the Diary of Johann Hauser's *Woman* (1985)
- 89 Just Another Typical Day
- 90 The Archaic Body
- 92 A Brief History of Getting Naked
- 94 Coney Island, October 2008
- 95 Freaks
- 97 John Ashbery, I Want You to Keep Whispering Your Sweet Nothings in My Ear Forever or a Valentine's Day Poem to Poetry
- 98 If Eliot Were to Write Your Personal Apocalypse

- 101 *Acknowledgements*
- 103 *Notes*

A PRELUDE

Found poem taken from a letter picked up in the street dated October 14, 1989, otherwise known as "Art, I was foolish."

Dear Art –

I always foolishly listen to you.
Art, you talk nothing but BS.
I foolishly told people where I came from and where I had been.
Did you ever warn me not to?
No, Art.

You never say or do anything constructive
that would help my life.
Then you foolishly expect me to thank you.
For what, Art?
You never did anything for me.

You foolishly told me.
You foolishly kept me there.
That's why I have nothing but a miserable old age.
Thanks to your foolish advice and your foolish blunders.
I worked my fool head off, but you let it all go

down the drain, Art.
You even kept making me throw my good clothes away!
You are to blame for all my troubles in life, Art.
Before I knew you, I was happy-go-lucky.
After I knew you, my life became a hell on earth.

Had I stayed in Athabasca and not come running
to you like a damn fool.
I was being a fool to stay there and a bigger fool
to listen to anything you said.
Art, you only ever wanted a pigsty for me.

You have no brains, Art.
The truth is, you wanted me to live
on a mere pittance.
It's such a tragedy.
I could have been making big money.

But I'm not – all because of your damn foolishness.
You had no sense, Art.
I listened to you and it was a BIG TRAGEDY!
Art, don't contact me again.
Dorothy.

POEMS
THAT WERE
OVERHEARD
IN VARIOUS
LOCALES

DECOUPAGE

And so they come a-courting in the Greyhound depot,
those torn bits of boys, those wanton travellers,
having won a fuzzy, bedizened animal

from the Hunter and Gatherer machine.
A claw descends with the exuberant morbidity of children
who play Barbie and Ken, Cannibals beneath the dining-

room table as the compote and endives are served.
There's always a more precisely foreign term for life's
sticking-together of things, a lilt that boosts the ego

in all the unHeimlich lands of Sturm und Drang we must
pass through, sons with guts busting the glitter glue off
their *Dukes of Hazzard* tees as they glut themselves

with filet-mignon Doritos, old ladies who do Sudoku
like sex, older ladies in fur, awkwardly lavish velour gowns
with Uggs. There's just a five-minute stopover in every

small town in Canada, long enough to buy a dream catcher,
to chat about your tubal ligation with a complete stranger,
almost a *de rigueur* pas de deux à la five a.m., Valentine's Day,

the edges pasted down so finely I can barely see where the piazza
meets Dali's *Persistence of Memory*, where the Tower of Pisa leans
into Blake's "Sick Rose," only a hand reaching out mutely

to gift me with a panda, and the oldest lady of all yelling out,
"Really, at this point, I'd rather walk."

THE DILDO CRAFTSMAN

Other men when they retire go into
the tying of lures, the carving
of decoy ducks, doing Sudoku
hour after hour, fiddling
with rebel trucks, he though,
"nearly a hundred years old,"
says the cashier at Womyns' Ware,
went instead into the manufacture
of sex toys, pouring hot rubber
into ridged molds, each individualized,
6.5 inches long, 3 inches wide, a range of sizes
and monikers, from Beginner's Delight
to the Monster, his most popular line
the three perfectly proportioned dongs
known as Ladies' Choice, each with
its own carrying case, every schlong
marked by subtle flaws that almost
make them flesh despite their night-black,
lilac and Bubblicious-pink hues, all,
the cashier adds, "delicately scented
with the smell of linseed oil" that the ancient man
uses to slick each dildo from its unique
frame, his memory reciting moments
perhaps, of being young, when he was
this ready to enter and remain, every shaft
his gift to the women who were
or could have been, imagining,
as he loosens each cooled replica,
the hands that will touch it after his,
positioning it at the opening,
pushing it deeper.

THREE OVERHEARD SONNETS

I. NINETEENTH CENTURY FEMALES

I mean she has nothing! No real estate –
two well-pearled Götterdämmerungs hissing
on the platform, purses a-hooked over furs, fate
vacuum packed in formal cortical zones, missing

little – they think – hideously decisive, never
knowing plonk or dive or Money Mart advances,
always supremely heeled, primed for endeavours,
no yee-haw or la-di-da or zip-a-dee-doo chances

to fail – all is planned – right down to their plots
in the chi-chi cemetery where their associates
may visit with slim dabbings of the eye or, more likely, not.
My great-grandmother was one of them, sure the ingrates

would bring babies to her funeral, specifying in her will
no crying infants admitted, in fact, no children allowed at all.

2. TWENTY-FIRST CENTURY CONSUMERS

Sandra said the python felt like white silk;
we took her word for it. Who can gauge
reptiles in a business suit anyway; creatures of that ilk
best judged in the nude, according to *GQ*, far beyond the cage

of antique Rolodex and the latest iPhone. Still
we were taken aback, in private, that one of us,
we thought, had so transgressed against the daily drill
as to descend into that world of incipient death and lust

on her week off, choosing to book a tryst with a snake
instead of a vacay normalized and dull, something we
could get, Cabo or Fort Lauderdale perhaps, it was spring break
after all, and who was Sandra to us now the key

to her was gone, Mastercard, we bet, had already put a hold
on her credit, snakes exceeding her limit and she so far beyond the fold.

3. TWENTIETH CENTURY VICTIMS

*That's all she needs on her last day –
a bomb threat and to be taken hostage,* what
a climax after forty years of cashiering at Save-
On-Everything, the World's Biggest Dollar Store. Got

a buck or slightly more? We have it all:
discount Shih Tzus, somewhat-worn Belle Dames
avec or sans merci, breech-born *Übermensches*, tall
but awkward courtiers, rather dented Lambs

of God, a whole panoply of life forms, only for
a loonie and a bit – what could be more just
and now these terrorists have Connie bad, like a whore
on sale, roped up in the back, and we can't bust

her loose. As sadly, the bomb tick tick ticks and when you
come right down to it, I guess her payment to obliteration's due.

RESIDUAL LINGERIE

On the Amtrak from Portland to Vancouver

Cape Intrepid and the kite receding, slam slam slam through the boxcar slits. Here we are hybrid; here we are indigent; travelling two to each side with our packets of mayonnaise, our filched wine, the violence of incessant sandwiches. Ladies who go shopping most everywhere have unclear lexicons for the landscape.

The beach is indeed most "beachy" as they cluck and on the screen the Mima Mounds, "evenly spaced lumps of dirt" located somewhere around Tukwila are gushed over as "joyous mysteries." True it is all that and more, yes when the sun's extreme veils surge down upon us and suddenly a whole fleet of tiny kin sailboats

rear up like silver, pale sabres of isolate ships is the line inscribed tragic as ink in my mind, the human race in sum, so much glowing continuing apace while we subscribe to the impossible recollections of the lens, wanting hard to hold the keel and mast in us forever.

THIRLED

And so I pass the place again where he stuck his fingers
up me and stole my bus ticket.
"I want to sit beside the snail," a boy whines in the breakfast nook
at the Travelodge in Barrie.
There is a certain *je ne sais quoi* in imagining one is Frank O'Hara

at the end of a long hard day testing the stretchability
of condoms in Roussillon, France. Yes,
there are jobs like this and others involving 418
interchangeable plastic parts like when I pass the place again
where he stuck his fingers up me and stole my bus ticket

and remember that I never ate at Helen's Grill;
not even their famous hamburger.
Grief does this to you;
it gives you back and takes away your hunger until
there is a certain *je ne sais quoi* in imagining one is Frank O'Hara

simply lounging, *flâneur*, slacks casually pleated
and an umpteenth cigarette lodged between your lips,
nothing sordid in this, little vulnerable either,
as when I pass the place again where he stuck his fingers up me
and stole my bus ticket;

the beginnings of revision, you might say, of repetition,
of an unestablishable loss,
like the goat who loved a burro or the longings behind vaginoplasty.
O yes, there is a certain *je ne sais quoi*
in imagining one is Frank O'Hara.

As the NBA announcer says into the camera,
"Butch, we just have to deal with it," I believe he really
did relegate the emotions of childhood to this sound bite,
this certain *je ne sais quoi* of imagining
one is Frank O'Hara

while I pass the place again
where he stuck his fingers up me, then stole my
bus ticket.

BIBLE STUDY GROUP AT THE BEACH

He is bald and stocky and a Warren; and the surfer kid
is Corvid; blue bikini girl, Shannon; while the guy
hoodied in the sand is Darren and unmoving – eighteen of them
piping names and their favourite things to do, top among
these, sleeping. Vince spouts: "I like to dream about myself
sleeping," while Jay cracks, "But is the you sleeping
in your dream also having a dream about sleeping?"
Nathan then adding, "Sleeping? Forget it. I like to
travel to Antarctica every weekend and set up
utopias with all the penguins." Nubile surrealism.
So far so good. Then Warren opens Thessalonians,
along with a bag of cookies, a vat of iced tea, and
the riches begin, for this is today's sermon, Christ's
great wealth of love, and gradually the kids turn like clock
hands away from him, skipping rocks into the ocean,
gazing towards the near-flint of sunset: "We don't have
to worry about a thing, children," Warren blissfully intones,
"because Jesus is in us, in our every act and word," and I think
of the old mechanic on the Greyhound to Campbell River
who told me his wife spends her days running a "small
farm on the computer" and is indeed "perfectly happy."

A LITTLE NOTE ON PASSING BY

For us it's fine the forests are empty
and the seas are merely picturesque residue.

We have been taught appearance is everything
and cannot resign our mirrors now.

The train is five minutes away from Oshawa
and on the first Metro of the morning

a man called Raymond ate a sandwich, crumbs
constellating his overalls.

We are thanked for depositing our garbage
in the bin but have no idea where it goes

and enjoy our beautiful ignorance.
Why not write a Frank O'Hara poem?

Sometimes life is just a series of events
with filaments less than more connecting.

Like now when I am served my soup
in a random Scottish pub and ask for only

a small amount of pepper while it starts
to snow thin as litter and a woman pronounces

certain as Li Po: "It's the intelligent people
that are truly dangerous when they're stupid."

OCEAN, A PERSONAL AD

"You look better if you don't smile too big in photographs,"
the aging woman notes, pondering how much more Botox
to insert into her coin-operated dispensing machine.
Hey, I have nothing against whatever you want to do to your

carrying case for the spirit. In autocorrect how quickly I become
Casanova or Caruso after all and there are no solid ways to fix
the ebb and flow of my personal ocean.
Why the paramour is so often a brick wall with just a small

window of desire in it is worth discussing under the title
of Childhood's Nine-to-Five Jobs, one of which might have been
bus driver or Lord of the Road as he tells us, formally, to call him,
on the rainy highway to Parksville. "It's part of my charm," he insists,

to often have none, I mean I wouldn't
want you to get used to too much ice cream on Sundays.
Agreed, I guess. Everything dies, right, so it's best that ashes
lie upon each surface from the get-go,

even the slippery veneer of your pulsating and flawed heart.

JUST THE WAY THINGS ARE (HE SAID)

That day at the tracks was overcast.
We cheered for a filly called Morning Coffee
and then Swagger Cat went down and had to be shot.

At the pub, the dealer wore a bandana beneath a dark fedora.
"It's the law of supply, you know," he said.
Two men played soccer in the cemetery beneath the train,

white ball pinging off the old grey of graves.
The horse went down as it graced a curve with its hooves,
and when it tried to rise, its leg was a shred of skin.

At the Met, the dealer moved a scrim in front of it
and slowly the hearse that smelled of hay drew towards us.
A ball bounced between our tables on which were placed small

shooters of blood. "I clean my asshole with Baby Wipes," the dealer
piped up, "that's the kind of pure guy I am." Graves took on the rain again
as they had for the past century. At the track, the crowd gasped,

briefly, then pretended their vision of glory hadn't
just been shattered as #5 racehorse was loaded cold
into the law of demand.

POEMS THAT WORK IN THE TV WORLD

MOVIE INDUSTRY TRASH

Gak gak gak until the smooth hoods of plastic bags have slid
into each placed can, been crimped about the rim
and every handle eared with a tight loop of green – one
for breakfast, one for sandwiches, another for lunch, a last
perhaps for hot snack or just because Teamster Bob
driving Star Trailer A chooses to ditch twelve boxes of
Frito-Lays he's been storing up, spilling them
onto the asphalt, then the canisters of atmospheric gas
clearly labelled *Danger* set rolling down the long circus path
where they were tossed but fast tip them in too along with,
cut, the sharp bands around signs, tossed earplugs, pink tape
laced about cable, rubber bands, oil rags, gel squares and fly
into set with a broom to clean the explosion on Scene 83,
Apple, Take One where a window/door/room shatters,
disgorges and glass, real or rubber, constellates the floor
or there has been a skirmish of the hero against
evil, that endless battle, and a machine-gunned wealth of shells
must be herded into cups cups cups, cast down everywhere,
momentary paper containments for bad java
slammed on any convenient shelf then replaced an hour later
with another amnesiac brew, or those paper plates with dismissed
remnants, left on the day or at call or by the Abby shot
whole platters of muffins, rolled rugs of cold cuts slid into pails,
wasted, so fall in and do the rounds with a butt sweep where
especially about the work trucks you will locate middens of darts
to tip in yet another bin, which at wrap wrap wrap will be knotted up
and Steve or Dave or Dan will cart them off, hundreds
of takes and it's a walkway again.
GACK!

SHOOTING AFGHANISTAN IN MINATY BAY

Five refugees stand on their marks,
clad by Wardrobe in muslin rags, laden
by Props in tin pans, water canisters,
empty rucksacks hoisted to their shoulders with rope.

A sketch is sufficient – four tarpaulin huts,
two armored trucks, a triad of flags,
the ubiquitous oil cans and all that sand in soiled
mounds, lit to look like winter.

The soldiers hold the guns.

All day long, the sniper dies,
the turfed people straggle about the camp,
an engine revs and cuts.
We are full of majestic ennui

in our world of make-believe, somewhere in the real
mountains of BC, a little chilly today,
the catfish overcooked, the ravens we started
at first light with now flying

far from this incomprehensible difference between making art and war.

THE STASH

for Jeff

Gels, duves, flaps, tabs –
tables glittered with bits
of jewel-hued plastic –
scarlet, blue, white-flame
green or black flops,
bulldogged, chloroplasts.

Twelve plus hours a day, the rhythm
is this: measure, slice, cease
as the roll holds, stuck still
in Times Square mime montages
or squatting to apple box or
tippy cart until "CUT!"

After, the hands resume,
soft machines of anticipation,
waiting the Blonde they
will demand, the Long Arm,
the Shotgun, the Chimera –
atomics scatter to set – copy,

copy, got it – flying in.

THESE ARE THE CONDITIONS

Not simply rain but all the world's water,
relentless and tremendous upon the slicker-clad
crew as the rush is on us to set up now. Two a.m.

another fourteen-hour camera day, meaning eighteen plus
for Locations, o department of slog and sweep away.
Quick the village is on the move, there, no, there, no,

heft the tent again, one on each metal limb, over
the embankment and down the berm to stick it
fast in the mud and Velcro tight the walls heavy

with wet, like pasting up sheets of old chewing gum.
Brockton Point where the goons will stage a shootout,
Yvan on B-cam sliding on the rails to zoom in, the villain

slamming out in a limo and still it teems, pretties struggling
to do checks with powder and pen beneath a massive fly swatter
weighed with bags about which the deluge spatters while ducks,

indifferent to our trucks, three-holer, traffic lock-up with barricades and
wand, continue to winch the cove open with quacks, the home of my
birth a backdrop for a certain kind of perfect suffering.

TWO A.M., AFTER TAKING HOURS TO SHOOT THE FINAL SCENE, NORTH VAN MEMORIAL GROUNDS

Who knows how long they have been shooting the rendezvous between the werewolf

    and the transvestite?

Loopy Loo's feet are two heavyweight champions from hell as she stands locking up traffic

    from the circus

to the tombstones with her clown-nosed dildo and the face of a smiling pylon. When o when will

    it be turnaround

on the Abby shot and then the blessed Window set-up? Jill has wheeled out the tiny

    hamburglets with squirts

of hot sauce; the honey wagon reeks of Febreze; a processional of teamsters line the route to

    receive all those empty

propane canisters. It's raining again. Small gelid spores clustering on the backs of dead leaves

    and L. L. wonders

what James Fayden McCayley thinks of all this tromping about on his grave, he who

    died at thirty

in 1926 and is commemorated by an exquisite stone mandolin, his era's ubiquitous willow that

    weeps.

JUST ANOTHER DAY IN FILM

The BGs are restless.
Five o'clock in a fake street in faux Hong Kong
and there is some concern about the repetition of umbrellas.
AD Mr. K sports his *Day of the Dead* button-down
and asks Crafty if we've been "abandoned.
What no meat and cheese platter by two a.m.?"
No, just the torturous scent of ham wafting
over Oceanic Plaza as the lone paparazzo
attempts to get an apropos angle
on the erstwhile superhero, looky loos
huddle on the fringes of the cast tent, desperate
for a boo at stardom and the wardrobe
ladies remain aghast they've allowed "two salmons"
to appear on screen together.
But this is later.
Now we are in Hong Kong as represented
by strings of laundry, colourful pinwheel vendors
and no bike helmets, where an "insert on the knife stabbing"
is projected pre-turnaround and the inappropriate security guard
watching the camera cart is sharing his near heart attack
from blow with me, his recent tremor from Cialis
while "screwing this five-hundred-dollar ho."
I hate to tell you more of what I must listen to
as I stand on the edge of nothingness licking a Klondike ice cream.
Someone thrust it into my hand
as if I were a garburator at a birthday party.
I had no choice.
Now you see what I mean.

THE DECEASED BGS

Their blood is delivered in pizza boxes, nine layers deep, Rorschachs of rubber, ruby-hued amoebas, slapped down on the cement beneath where they swing

from chains in a pseudo-drug den, all their bling a chandelier of redundancy. You see them at Crafty, slathered with latex contusions, and suddenly lose interest

in jelly donuts for life. In Holding, they tilt on chairs, texting the living, not quite zombies but more the recently deceased with their inability to recognize

boundaries, their sweet self-torturing. As one corpse dangles from a noose, last scene, cornstarched cocaine snowing down, near rolling, his phone rings,

his wife has just given birth, and the crew gathers around the killed man, applauding again and again, the juxtaposition, the miracle.

CAST DRIVER FOR NUMBER ONE

Davidovich looks at the moon, its orbicular ruin,

and something secondary leaves his eyes;

the primary rises. Here,

over the river, where he waits in his Mercedes

to be called, a reimbursed servant to Number One's strut,

his ache for takeout from Bing-Wah,

a yearning for private moments in the trailer – his child

on Skype and all his hours attendant to network

happiness. Davidovich snitches

this instant of beauty, then "Kenny will have his nut!"

he whips out loudly at the run-ragged crew

who cannot ensure every

take will be reverent, unmarred by sudden bogeys

or life-preserving chat, his Number One

disgruntled later at the lack of respect,

hunched in the leather bucket seats on the drive

to the manse, fans left straggling back

to Chilliwack, their moment of access

to the stars left unrecorded beneath the moon's

ruthless, soothing indifference.

WHEN I LOVE FILM THE MOST

is in the dark hours
in a warehouse or studio
held in the twilight of making,

all outside us night and within, the lamps,
actors rehearsing their Shakespearean
hunger, mock slaying each other with swords,

parkouring over the set dec landscapes, then,
between rolls, Patrick, the sound guy,
might cue a tune on his laptop

(Spandau Ballet, Sinatra); Nathan,
stand-in, will play shadow puppets against
a flop; the grips powwow on apple boxes;

Gil, genny op, juggles eggs; Bill asks,
"what was your favourite past life?"
When I love film the most is the time

we have worked twelve or more hours
on aching feet, schlepped endlessly,
been drenched in the downpour and still,

a cheerfulness remains, as if we are all
a playful child made of component parts:
one the mouth that blows bubbles, another

the hands cat's cradling, the next, legs
skipping. One person in that instant, gorgeous,
exhausted, but as a baby is, without regrets.

POEMS THAT ATTEND TO FAMILIAR CHARACTERS FROM THE PAST

WASHING

Two inches. All the water we were allowed
in the tub. My father's orders.
Four of us, aged three to ten, bleached sugar peas
in our porcelain pod, shoulders
and thighs stuck together, small buttocks dipped
with water like the tips of Dairy Queen cones,
the kind we were bought once a year as a bribe
following the family photo session

at Brown's on Kingsway. We could never
luxuriate. He wouldn't permit such wastefulness.
The water wasn't even hot, but a pissy-warm
puddle we crouched in, slathering cloths
swiped with thin ridges of soap over our limbs, slapping
the cotton squares against spines and knees,
damp flags of cleanliness. Our mother officiated
at the bath, here squidging a comma of Johnson's No

More Tears shampoo onto a plastered-down scalp,
there slopping a plastic cup of water over a frothy head
in her skint benediction. Though at the end
of bath time she would drape a towel over her lap
and the younger ones would leap into that soft pocket,
a plush and highly coveted moment, this
was meagre consolation. Even our rubber duck was grim,
its yellow promise never allowed

to bob, jammed as it was among our collective feet, moored.
When, years later, I travelled to Turkey
it was to learn how to yield to water.
On my first day in Cappadocia, I sought out a *hammam* where,
for twenty-five euros, a woman wearing a white kerchief and pure apron
washed me.
Languishing on a heated stone in the *sıcaklık* as she squeezed
a cheesecloth of minty suds over my prone body,
I became a child again,

that fantasized child I had never been,
who could eat as much as she desired without
a careful doling out, wear the clothes she longed for, indifferent
to budget, sink into the endless depths
of hot water without guilt. Just for awhile anyway.
"*Çok güzel*," the woman murmured, her olive gaze
drenching me where I lay. *Yes, indeed. So beautiful.*
As the water dripped down upon me, unskimpingly, into the light.

THE WINDOW WASHER

for Patrick

Since eighteen he's been doing this and still feels fear
strapped in his thin harness rappelling down
or riding reflected clouds on the deck of the boom lift
regardless of wind, heat, any kind of weather
his job to shine the windows clear
to return a transparence to what can be seen.

It's what he first liked, making people see,
scraping grime and droppings from neglected views, fear
not stopping him from washing til they were clear
glass after glass echoing his progress down
until whether he was cleaning so they could see him, or whether
this work had made him invisible, a spectre on a lift,

he couldn't say. Twenty years already on this lift,
in Vancouver, Williams Lake, Whistler, see
after high school's impossible stillness, he knew whether
mountain biking or skydiving, he'd be on the move, fear
never anything that held him back, so down
since his mother's death when he was twelve, it was clear

he'd never amount to much, his father said, clear
that cunt and drugs would be his lot, he'd never lift
himself above them, end up dying down
on skid row like the other half-breed punks, you see
his mother had been hit by a truck one New Year's, his fear
pumped into darkness worse than any weather

he now faces dangling from these wild ropes, weather
that swings him like a puppet as he's getting in the clear,
bashes him into his bucket, walls, fear
submerged in survival, excitement, the lift
he gets from wrangling with the blacker gods, seeing
it through, refusing to rappel down

until every last window is clean, down
to the difficult seams and crevices, the edges, whether
he has to use a pole or a cloth with ammonia, seeing
through that glass is paramount, all the surfaces clear;
he likes to imagine the workers in each tower, the lift
they get from viewing each clean vista, revealed, beyond fear.

No time for fear, he thinks, going down in the boom lift
whether each glass is clear, that's all, really, that can be seen.

JIGGER

Looking at Mahsoud, short but concealing a muscled arsenal
beneath that button-down shirt, the scent of a practised seducer
despite his sloping pupil, an eye lazy as egg white in his face, I

shrink. It is raining or I never would have come here.
Not just drizzling but a torrent of wet that slashes the surface of the Bosporus,
driving the bridge fishers home, that cascades over Taksim

Square's marquees and the endless blatting of horns, Simit Sarayı about
to close. I had tossed down the last of the Nescafé, crumpled up the wax paper
from one of their pasty buns, crammed with cheese or

spinach or jam, hefted the damp bag on my shoulder again, three a.m. and
where, not in possession of four hundred euros for a room, would I go? Plumping
my jacket beneath my head, just under the partial covering

of an awning, four hours until dawn, I had been nearly asnooze when
the policeman shook my arm. "Kanadoleum," is all I thought to gasp
in my approximate Turkish, as if a Northern status

condones dossing down on the pavement. They call Canada "that cold
heaven" my Turkish friends warned before I left;
androgynous and innocent, I had planned to conquer everything,

not knowing, a woman alone, I am viewed only as easy, rich.
The cop had merely wanted me to move along, no other interest
in my well-being, just concerned, as in the vacuity of all big cities,

that tourists not witness vagabonds. So I had begun to walk.
Too many cats, I later recalled, clinging like *kargas*
to drainpipes, the cusps of roofs, skirting the traffic circle,

nursing their perilous babies beneath the giant letters of the Levi's sign.
And then Mahsoud had been there, beckoning in that deceptive
haven of English – "Excuse me, miss, but do you need some help?"

It is Hasan's fault I later decide, my lover's, the reason I was there,
for being so different – his slowed beauty, sullen shyness, impossibly
quiet longings failing to prepare me for the more regular gregariousness,

the crude flirtations and, harder, the insistence masquerading as
hospitality. Yet, I was cold, tired and wet. "Nowhere is open anymore
to get *kahve* or even *su*," he claimed, strolling

beside me, the proffered umbrella floating above our heads.
"I have a place, though, comfortable, small, but you can sleep, promise,
a pleasure to assist a Canadian, really." My national pride had risen,

sewn as tightly inside me as the patch on my pack, and I had agreed.
Once in, of course, too late. His suite not tastefully furnished;
a shoe rack in the front hall of the three-storey walk-up, narrow sofa

in the den, a stack of videos – *Barbarella, When Harry Met Sally*
– the only knick-knacks I see a set of *matryshkas*,
usually slipped one within the other, but here placed in order

of ascending height on a whitewashed shelf. "O a girlfriend
gave me those. A Russian. She lived with me awhile."
It is only long after, staying with the lawyer from Beyoğlu who

took pity on me, a girl without a passport, broke, that I
hear of The Natashas, a name that conjures up a bad pop band
but refers to sex slaves from the Steppes, blonde-haired girls

lured to Turkey by work, kept, sometimes as long as ten years
before their bodies are found. If I'd only known this story before
then I would have choked up my food allowance for a room,

my traveller's cheapness be damned. Instead, I was only
cautioned to watch my drinks at bars, keep ID on me at all times.
And so now I pay attention as, in the box of his kitchen, Mahsoud

pours us tea, hot water slamming over the rim of pale mugs,
the tea bags, cinnamon peach, bobbing on top. "Cookies?" he asks,
playing the saviour. And after we have finished sipping, I resist

when he shoves a pair of folded gray pajamas at me,
barks more gruffly, "Shower, girl, then change into these."
I check my money belt: lira, a passport, smile around a surge of ire,

"O no, I couldn't. So sleepy. Just need to rest."
His features suddenly seizing into a simmer
on the edge of dangerous, "But you will make me angry.

I am trying to be kind. Come now. I insist." His sharp arms urging
me towards the bathroom where he turns on the shower, tests
the heat. "See. This feels nice. Just relax. Get clean now."

The door doesn't lock. I stand there awhile, the water
draining, holding the institutional nightwear, certain
there is no way I will get naked, not willingly.

A year before, I had first stripped in front of Hasan,
he gazing from the couch as I stood, slightly disgraced,
sticking out the small points of my breasts,

cupping my pudenda, then finally moving towards his belt,
as though asleep with desire, releasing the strange solitude
of his cock and taking it between my lips while he hardly shifted,

barely moaned, a taciturn horniness I could never fathom,
never stir him beyond. Now I exit the stark
square of the bathroom, decline once more, phrasing my refusal

carefully, afraid of incurring threats. "It's simply not my custom,"
I try. "In Canada we don't shower at stranger's houses. So can
you show me the room?" He has been staring out the window,

a plot of darkness in the wall, facing nothing. "But crazy girls
from Canada go to stranger's houses?" he remarks, sour
laughter in his words as he gestures towards the door.

"Sleep in there. On top of the sheets. I'll be out here then."
The room is white and red. Teddy bears
everywhere and the satin duvet quilted with

Seni Seviyorum – I love you. Of course I know I won't rest,
would have been better walking the streets. Feigning
slumber, I hug myself to protect my stash of what

is now freedom, identity, wondering how much longer
until light. Before long, I hear the door swish open
over the too-thick pile of carpet and then Mahsoud is in the bed.

STEVE KULASH, TAXIDERMIST

Nostalgia is unethical.

If this is finally the end of my childhood.

On Kingsway, the taxidermist's shuts down, display

cases of skulls, dust-stuffed quails and white-tailed deer

emptied out.

I loved those windows of death.

This is how you get old, saying where are the merry-go-rounds.

Life always takes more of a risk back then.

Is neon or crinoline or salmon bloodying the banks

with their too-muchness.

Drawers and drawers of glass eyeballs; plastic claws by the bucketful.

If the imagination accretes around this.

If this is finally the end of my childhood.

I apologize for the lack of romance.

Memory has an immoral tinge.

It wants its cold beasts to worship.

JUST ANOTHER CHARACTER IN THE SONG OF SONGS

for my beloved dog parents, JR and FS

So the Egg Man cometh to Joe and Faye's as Faye,
in her tatty dressing gown
stands amid the camellias and wild onions feeding
the great dark birds of Qualicum
with damp cat kibbles, leftover filet mignon and stoops of pale bread,
the Egg Man
lopeth through the yard with a sack of raw chickens
in one hand, the other bearing
aloft his shimmering dozen, twelve luminous globes,
while Joe mumbles something
about Leonard Cohen's acid in Toronto, '66 or thereabouts,
a bucket of compost in one paw and his cane in the other,
waving like a snake with rigor mortis
as the coons gather around the TV
to watch a Judy Garland biopic
and harrumph in chorus,
the Egg Man,
having aced his harp solo in church that morning, now
lollops down the path, balletic of form,
despite his sleek pate, recently a winner of the one hundred metre dash
and now Madame F sits at her piano, playing études,
eggs, gripping the sun, already a-sizzle in the cast-iron pan.

THE JOURNAL OF JOHN BERRYMAN FROM 1948 TO 1971: A REVERSE GLOSA OF FIRST LINES

I don't know what happened all that summer
in the heat of Princeton, I became a loner,
overly fascinated by myself, my first downfall,
the small infidelities that lead to larger, the poems
that open the path to what's always hungry and then I was dumber
than with Beryl in Heidelberg, that once-soft
pledge to the flesh, how it fit like something questionless
and opiate, quelling the ghosts, making me calmer
than I'd been in a good long while, since before Ma became
Jill Angel and Father shot itinerancy to silence, when I wrote,

"I am the same yes as you others, only,"
and let it trail off, forgot whom I was ranting to, another lonely
attempt to define the what of self, not long after
Dylan died at St. V's and the St. Pancras dreams began,
full of as many hooded beings as Magritte, wholly
drenched with the fantastic disappearances of love, Mistress
Bradstreet's pangs, the sharp salt-tack of absence.
I believe in my mind, must I apologize for this, even faintly,
even between the pages of night? It is not all intoxicant,
this life, there is much that must remain murk, inexplicable and now

I do not show my work to anybody, I am quite alone,
I keep my befuddlings to myself, the strange way they emerge, my antique tone,
even when bound into a book, it all seems to remain private,
incommunicable as music heard in the blue hour of dawn,
no different than if I was presented in a shroud, my lips sewn,
standing behind the mute podium to receive an award of dirt.
What's all this to Twissy anyway, a poem compared to a child?
She coos and sucks and meets the world with unafflicted eyes, shines
loud. Though her sad padre profanes, gets soused and dries out again
like a poisonous plant, she, oblivious, forgiving though I rage,

"I put those things there. – see them burn."
That's what I want, to fire the sight, for all and once to turn
wordings to ash. The god of rescue worms up in me, promises
a sobriety without violence but am I capable and more,
will the poems divest me or worse, now and with permanence, spurn
my frail attempts to hear them? Another one is born; another one,
but the Biblical name is no proof of eternity. Though I'll attend
the christening, I walk still too much by the bridge, wonder if I will learn
before the final crescendo descent, something, what,
I'm not sure, but there is water in it and a moving towards the bright.

WHAT I REMEMBER ABOUT ATTENDING ELEMENTARY SCHOOL

It was to be momentous: The Adventure Playground. Instead,
I hunched in the corner with stacks of books, played with a handkerchief
I'd dubbed Mehitabel.
That was the hobby
and the crusade? Dandelions.
How they must be saved.
Still I wasn't a total pariah, could sneak
cinnamon toast and Scooby-Doo from one girl,
buy the rest off with chocolate squares at grade four camp
where I pretended to have breasts and was that before or after we learned
about the Mi'kmaqs? A velour dress; a bowl cut; the hapless violin.
Occupied our time making clay totem poles,
singing "Leaving on a Jet Plane" as I imagined I was blind or allergic
or sick or lame. Mostly, wrote. And then the Catholic grief began:
scritchy grey skirt, nuns. All my dreams in French.
Tetherball; bake sales; a little drool over the altar boys between
being spat on by the Phillipina gang
at the gates. What did we learn?
There were maps, diagrams, a computer we plonked
the arrow keys on, other vague accoutrements of education.
Mostly, it was suffering.
Of the stupid, untranslatable, apocalyptic kind.
They would never understand the pain of multiplication tables,
nor of being forced to ride a tiny tricycle on Sports Day, nor of being teased
for one's unfixable face, or worse,
the agony of seeing Nabil's nipple beneath his shirt and it being
as far away from touch as the resurrected Christ.

WHAT I REMEMBER ABOUT BEING BORN

That it doesn't cease. The horror and the scrumptiousness of it.
My father snapping artsy photos of my head crowning, dark moon
within a ring, through the smeared surgical mirror.
That it was long.
Days contracted, released as my mother walked, lay,
knew stirrups, pushed. Summer outside, all the imminent sandcastles.
Two weeks past a given date for exposure and naming.
That she was pressured. To expel me.
To take the drip drip drip of induction into her veins
in order not to get larger, more conspicuous.
And when I was slow, still, to acknowledge forceps.
As I loved the dim passageway where I dreamed.
Yet they wouldn't let me linger. Dented
my soft fontanelle to say today the light will tear at your eyes
and the cord be cast aside into a suitable garbage pail. Someone cried.
I'd like to tell you it was my father though this is likely conjecture or longing
as, in his scrubs, so young, he looked besotted instead.
My mother getting stitched outside the lens. I suckling the breasts
she refused to bind, her nipples remaining virginal, the night's
antiseptic reverence descending on the ward, then, the world.

WHAT I REMEMBER ABOUT WHAT WE WEREN'T ALLOWED IN CHILDHOOD

Pop-Tarts certainly. Anything processed. The worst being hot dogs
which I gobbled once guiltily at the Stardust roller rink at thirteen
and puked, imagining entrails in my intestines. Condiments. Definitely
not on the acacia table in gauche plastic containers.
And Halloween candy was entirely out. My father sifting
through our sacks for all but the Glosette peanuts and Sun-Maid
raisins that, rationed, we were able to gobble over later weeks
to flee the dreaded sugar rush. Mostly all not carob or bean sprouts
or hard-boiled eggs were verboten. And then too there was no *Happy Days*,
never *Knight Rider* or *The Monkees* except when we snuck them
at Nana's by lying to her and after she would always exclaim
– "You pulled the wool right over my eyes!" So, aside from educational
programming, the small B & W stayed dark while we clicked Meccano
bits together, read the Brothers Grimm or played doctor with toothpaste.
Absolutely no Barbies or anything that would break, rot our teeth,
show us a false world in which dolls sport slip-on pink heels
and grown men in leather jackets say "Ehhhhh!" Only the dentist
could give us video games, hand-held Donkey Kong and Frogger
while he tightened our headgear, pain overwhelming the transgressive
pleasure and we couldn't say we didn't believe in God.

NINE: AN EXTENDED, SHORTENED CORONA

Getting old means the yearning to record
how once you were innocent, uncharred,
a stick-thing of a girl, no torment about having
or not having breasts, hips, legs that stretched
a certain lustable distance – no, this the age
where you remember exclaiming to your mother –
"why does that teen paint her nails when dirt
is much more glorious?" Glorious, OK, you may
not have used that word but still – the indignation,
bafflement, a longing for eternal androgyny – then.
Caught between fighting for the dandelions with your
hand-wrought placard – the only result – a shunning –
and the wooing of potential companions with chocolate
squares, baked in a glass pan and cut into solid blocks of hope –
they scorfed and then dismissed you – you with an imaginary
friend dubbed Mehitabel formed by a purply handkerchief,
you with your avid stack of books and gawky teeth –
not yet with the cruelty grade five would bring – spits and
taunts at the entryway – but nonetheless, an indifference.
You weren't as déclassé as K who had a bee tossed
in her mouth or D whom no one could be seen even
glancing at lest their sight became infected as lore went –
you had a thin circle of kin. The child of Jehovah's Witnesses
for instance, who could never do anything with you beyond
the classroom or the Jennifers behind whom you trailed,
sensing an incipient womanliness, a sportive joie de vivre
you could never approximate – worth playing the Dirty
Old Ogre to their chiffon-clad princesses to scent
the possibilities of togetherness – were you the pariah
you recall or just another kid with her weird foibles of that
particular age prior to hormones and their fuckery.

*

Particular age prior to hormones and their fuckery,
at nine you were not immune to rage, deceit, playing
la belle dame sans merci, palely loitering in bed,
pretending to be sick or ill but endlessly malingering,
once tonsils, bronchitis, pneumonia, now it was
a mysteriously chipped heel that, even once the cast
was removed – cocoon revealing the non-butterfly
of your yellowed and itched-up leg – refused to be whole.
Now you fell into a condition no one had known existed –
reflex sympathetic dystrophy – four children in all the world
whose limbs turned blue, cold and stiff – on emotional
provocation maybe? An ultrasensitivity? You remember
a satisfaction at tweaking adult anxiety, the comfort of weekly
visits to Doctors X and Y who sent you for tests involving blocks,
numbers, eventually concluded you were reading at a stupidly
high level, fitted you with gormless inserts in your shoes,
guaranteed, pre-braces and zits, to zap self-esteem into the pit
and you don't even know it happened, to this day.
Other than that *The Hobbit* in bed with an egg, narrow
soldiers of toast and the occasional PBS program on grammar
was imminently preferable to the everyday trek to school
and its brutalities. You were writing stories then, novels in which
each chapter was a page and the characters were all girls left
alone, escaped, gone wild to survive solo.
A world, in so many children, where they are abandoned and happy.

*

A world, in so many children, where they are abandoned and happy.
Which you certainly weren't, neglected that is, divested of anything,
but solitude, perhaps. Three siblings by then, two more daughters and the coveted
son (later, another). Nine years switching a former nun and an erstwhile architect
turned trucker into the total parental unit of Buster Brown decisions.
We would play instruments, however awfully, go to CCD for our
religious bumph beyond weekly church, learn French, eat organic,
read copiously and be served with a whack of culture: Yehudi Menuhin,
The Nutcracker, Jean Little reciting at the library, Robert Bateman at the gallery,
Itzhak Perlman, Yo-Yo Ma and a few summers, the Folk Fest – recalling little of this
but the heat, crowds and my refusal to use the Jiffy John for at least ten hours.
Somehow it all surged in, stuck, this diverse swash of making, and there
is no time where you do not recall wanting absence to become presence.
Once, in sudden anger over insult when you tipped your sister's head
with a fork in a fight, having to dash to your room and compose a poem
of sorts about ghost-holes and forgiveness, already knowing that
art is an offering even if one never gives it.

*

Art is an offering even if one never gives it – the verses,
tales piling up in soft exercise books with pale blue lines.
What you didn't write about at nine is what bears mentioning
though – how within your innocence – we didn't know what
hookers were, say, or why *bugger* was apparently a nasty word;
two years later it took nuns to first utter the concept of lesbianism
to us schoolgirls, who deduced it meant giggling around the lower
field, slapping each other's skirted asses with textbooks.
Yes, how inside the utter silence about violence and sex,
a madman was rampaging. That summer of my ninth year, he
was taking children whose names became a chime in my head –
Simon Partington, Darren Johnsrude – I won't give him the grace
of a christening – he would offer them jobs, the cliché of candy,
kittens he'd lost and would they help find them, then, what,
they vanished, bodies not yet found – all that lacuna for us
to play with. He drove a shiny blue car with silver wheels,
we decided, lived on the F level of the Burnaby Hospital
parking lot. Our games spun cannibal, predatory.
We tried to figure out loss without a lexicon to do so.

*

We tried to figure out loss without a lexicon to do so.
The first gerbil dead in my palm, I running down to the kitchen
to show the adults and they *awwww* and wrap it up quick,
pop it in a Kleenex box and bury it in the eventually
corpse-swarmed garden. The next gerbil a reincarnation
of sorts, bearing the same name. And one-legged Terry Fox,
not yet felled, hobbling purely for a cure along some cold
stretch of Canadian highway. Unlike the killer's, we cut his
picture from *The Province* my granddad got us to get when
he was visiting, at the corner store in the middle of the block
with its Lik-A-Stix, Popeye cigarettes, *MAD* magazines, milk,
Mr. Chan, taciturn, and the missus shuffling after us
as we poked the narrow aisles for the forbidden –
you buy, you buy, they barked and so we brought back
the funnies – *Broom-Hilda, Doonesbury* – and that picture
of Terry with his sweaty curls and fell in love with martyrdom.
Later that year, it was Lennon, shot by the rabid fan, his glasses
smashed on the pavement – iconic murder of signifiers – and I
crouching hours over the centrefold in the four-LP Beatles album
weeping, though I knew him not. I cried, too, about the last
unicorn in the Irish Rovers song.
Generally, I sensed the night in everything.

*

Generally, I sensed the night in everything.
Used to lie awake gazing at the ceiling until I saw
ships, tiny people, luminous miniatures, all setting
off for foreign parts, or I would stare at the green-and-yellow
curtains spackled with abstract white blooms until each false
flower became a face – some frightening – as was the thought
I sunk within that we are teensy specks in a darkened universe,
soon snuffed, and my small room shrunk with questions,
existentialist despair grown first in a fever I had at three when I dreamed
I was colouring a ladder to Heaven with silver and gold crayons and a voice
proclaimed, "If you go up you can't come down," a sign to live on,
I think, but since then a day a taint of knowledge that marked me as a child
only in form. At church, I focused on the blood becoming wine, the
incense and how wildly beautiful the body of Christ was, ectomorphic
on its cross, long-maned, only the slip of a loincloth between me
and further mysteries revealed. I knew there was no God and it
didn't scare me at all. Art being much already and nature a definite most
of what made me sing within myself, content.

*

Of what made me sing within myself, content, were trees, especially
the tall fabulist cedars in the front yard who told of crows and the wind
and were still climbable then, books slid out, devoured, tapped
back into shelves with a delicious click, and accretions of other things, too:
the little turtle, the ceramic pig, a bobble-headed geisha and, at the close
of grade four, the figurine Mr. Oscar Raasveldt made of himself clad
in graduation robes whose mortarboard later chipped and moustache sloped
off – small items I could line up, even Dentyne boxes with their satisfying
mansard caps, a whole row of them, along with phalanxes of plastic soldiers
and Indians obtained in packs from the dentist when I'd endured
another tooth removal or later, braces tightening, though
by that point it was more the thrill of hand-held Frogger or Donkey Kong.
Didn't think through the implications of tribes molded to their bows,
headdresses, thought I was Native myself – played it up by sporting a
silver headband jabbed through with a feather, responded to Hiawatha –
knew no one from non-European cultures
but one Asian girl and she was teased with the awful
ditty: "Me Chinese, me play joke, me put pee-pee in your Coke" – after
all we had toyed with being cannibals and didn't white, blonde Susanna get it worse,
her lunch kit plopped in the boys' urinals, Todd gleefully pissing on it – that
stinking *Dukes of Hazzard* container – why did she have this, we may have wondered,
and not a *Bionic Woman* one, say – a show I only watched at Nicole's as her mother
slept in, let us see whatever program we wanted behind the drawn curtain while
we munched on cinnamon toast and pretended to be Lee Majors; in a few years,
dreamed of David Hasselhoff. But that's not what made me happy at nine.
Writing everything did – a collection of witchy spells, tales of mannequins
coming to life, the Bible, abridged and narrated from the perspective
of an ant, insect gospel to shock those who claimed human pre-eminence.
Reverent sacrilege was how I remade my life.

*

Reverent sacrilege was how I remade my life. By this I mean what – that I told
lies in the cause of what made greater sense – the imagination's right.
So my father was a blind truck driver I said because he wore shades or
we were super poor and could only afford an ironing board to eat off
and stockings for toques. At six I even stole pockets of jewellery from
Drevant's and when caught, kept a silver key, insistent a priest
had given it to me (like a crow I was drawn to shine).
By nine it was being a witch or Native, then preteen, sporting
sudden breasts after finding a C-cup bra, always some elaboration
of what was not, twisted mystical and dramatic. At nine I felt it was
my world, these fabrications a material I'd chosen at least when I
couldn't refuse the duffle coat for Mass or worse, a pseudo-uncle's
lips when he bent to plant a wrong wet smooch on our small, confused
mouths. I couldn't stop the killer's rampage but I could write a spell
I insisted would split an enemy in two, in Summer become the Tlingit
Princess, abandoned by her people and rescued by a padre who fed me
bug juice as fists pounded Queen's "We Will Rock You" on the table at Latona's
Catholic Girls Camp on Gambier Island. Yes, I'm fitting the whole shebang
in that I recall of this time in which I still ate DQ cones after family photo sessions,
and knew all the neighbours by name: Mr. Morgan, Bernice, Lee and the Hansons,
before I dubbed my first crush at square dancing class, "Heaven," that vivid
bliss when, despite squabbles and illness, I was self, able to sink hard into a book or
a universe, invisible with intellect, witness and time.

*

A universe invisible with intellect, witness and time is what I had
the luxury to live within at nine on Spruce Street, not always, but
when I could, amid French, church, the gorgeous torture of violin
lessons in which "Lightly Row" was rewarded by a Smartie – yes, one –
or the refusal to bow "Ode to Spring" was punished at five by solitary
confinement in the teacher's room where I sucked my finger backwards
in silence, a transgression that led to headgear by eleven and remedial music
classes for the stressed where the glockenspiel replaced orchestral dreams.
Soon I was writing songs called "Hell Hole" and blasting Def Leppard,
strumming a Peavey T-13 after selling my five-piece drum kit
with its useless groovy whisks.
Nine, though, wasn't about music or the body per se but words,
my natural rambles curtailed by the killer, no more straying by the tiny
creek reading Bertha Morris Parker, nibbling Wheat Thins
and pressing leaves. The confinement began, the fear.
Being sick or scared called forth a need in me –
for language to encompass or transcend –
I didn't know which – just wrote – those limitations aching into sounds, forms.
Always there is this nine in me, that girl who was dirt and ink,
who swam in books and surfaced to breathe returned
until she got to this place where,
getting old, she still yearns to record.

SWALLOWS' NESTS OF ISLA DE JANITZIO, MICHOACÁN

Under the red cupola beside the cemetery, each bracket
slants in its backbone and the nests lean, fasten, every

mud-and-straw cup perfectly fit to its shadow, swallows slanting
through the mist over Lake Pátzcuaro, its volcanic shallows

where men with vast butterfly nets catch *pescado* and dream.
It is the Morning of the Dead. The Purépecha gather at dawn

below marigold *ofrenda*s, candles plunged between the blooms
and lit, baskets full of bland tamales, soft fruit draped with embroidered

cloths, set in rows on the etched stones. The tombs are swept,
washed; there is no weeping. And the swallows pass too over

the graveyard, in their beaks the thrashing white moths thought
to be the returning souls of lost children; the birds take them to

their accurate dark nests above the thick Janitzio cobblestones,
holding mouths that have opened around these rituals

for centuries, each nest a note plentifully tended, handed down.

JUST ANOTHER LOSS OF FAITH

Michoacán, Mexico
October 2011, **The Day of the Dead** *tour*

You'd been promised marigolds.
The brochures printed paradisiacal fields
full of ruffled buttery blooms and tourists
beaming amid these myriad suns, white skin flushed
with all the glory of fulfilling the dream.

But the Morelian farms were stripped.
As the guide achingly explained, a frost
had descended last week, white violator of travel
agency visions and most of the flowers were seized,
stalks flat on the thawing earth, only shrivelled fists of harvest

and now how would the shrines be loaded? How the debts paid?
The scent, so redolent it vanquishes decay, was
decay itself, and pale moths, the purported souls of the dead
bewildered the barren acreage, having nowhere apropos
to land. Thus we strayed between the huts where crones

in *rebozo*s bound radishes beneath icons of the Bleeding Heart
and there were no photo opportunities to speak of and none of us
were prepared for the heat, donkey shit smearing our sandals,
slashing off the failed itinerary, knowing for certain again
there is no God.

THE COMBINATION

The globe is mostly what I recall
how every long Sunday it was always there
when I soared the tallest while yet still small,

that it stood on what seemed to be a pivot of gold
which then rested firm on a green baize square
the sight of what we could never hope to hold.

Our faces staring up; I was allowed to make it spin
though my sister complained it wasn't really fair
as her head after all reached past my sharp chin.

Yet once the globe had begun its rickety whirl
the hush in the room left no sounds to spare
as we gaped at this orb, three church-dressed girls

watching Africa, China, then Russia soar past
their borders scar-prinked, their colours garish:
sherbet orange, mint pink and then the vast

Antarctic, whiter than our fears, a cream-
steeped strangeness we would dare to touch,
this land like a scream quenching treats for the good.

But I didn't much care and maybe never did as
the Earth had unlocked where the *Book of Lists* hid
and now Caligula and his freak show swarmed my mind's night lair.

MY PARENTS ARE PLAYING SCRABBLE ON THE DECK

My parents are playing Scrabble on the deck on a warm
May evening and I know even if my father isn't winning
he's anticipating victory; that he has taken far too much
time to place his latest word on the swivelling board,
while my mother, I know, is reading a book club novel,
something by Márquez or Moore and nibbling on a foil-
bared square of dark chocolate amid quick sips of rooibos
as the collie clicks around the long wooden table
and that when it's my mother's turn she will take haste to piece
her syllables, my father stealing this fast
moment to carry in the tea tray, to sneak in a Sudoku puzzle,
give advice on the spelling of *alluvial*, or just to gaze
over the ever-shifting yards that surround my parents' constant home.
O I know it is passing, that soon night will end the deep game again.

AGAINST BILLY COLLINS' REFUSAL TO READ POEMS CALLED "MY GRANDFATHER'S BINOCULARS"

Immediate deal-breakers . . . poems that seem obsessed with some object associated with a dead person: Grandpa's Toolbox . . . and the like. . . . How much poetic room such necro-fetishes are taking up these days.
BILLY COLLINS, Introduction, *Best American Poetry 2006*

He was no lecher; no birdwatcher according to family lore.
So why my grandfather kept this pair of binoculars – a Carl Zeiss
special featuring Porro prism lenses encased within a black pelvis,
eyepieces ringed with silver tracks and the four protective caps
still intact, its strap a thick leather, its case a nubbled crypt with puce
velour lining and a sturdy slide clasp – I don't know.
There was no deliberate passing on;
at some point they simply strayed into my possession
from his dispersed cache of middle-class status
symbols, perhaps all they were,
the binoculars squatting beside the oversized globe above the massive
family Bible, merely sigils of the fairly educated Anglican banker.
Yet, I'd like to think he did have cause for wonder, eager once
to owl them to his eyes and watch a distant-detailed world,
as I do when the small ships drift by and I want to mark their names,
to enter their fierce ceremony of water for awhile.

PROBLEMS WITH THE SENTIMENTAL PERSPECTIVE OVER A CONSTRUCTION SITE AND A NAZARETH CONCERT, CIRCA 2013

As a child she got maudlin over crushed pismires, that chartreuse
light of early morning and the Irish Rovers never going to see
no unicorn. Age simply shifts the mode of expression, embeds
a reticence to gush. Still, she lumps up watching the railway bridge
vanish daily behind rising rebar as if, because she is denied this view,
the structure ceases to exist in the world. And why must she
turn every construction worker him and so etch his loss in each
fluorescent vest or mosaic-stickered hard hat?
Even clinging to the triumphant hero narrative
is redundant once analyzed.
Dan McCafferty in his frail ivory button-down and twisted
angel pipes cranking on the taps
because he's old and obviously ill
and yet, betwixt slumps on the riser, he sings
as if for Eurydice's return (she writes) when really,
it's likely to pay for his emphysema meds
though why this is less noble or more banal has slipped her mind now
as truthfully she cannot stop trusting sigils that ping her tear ducts:
how steel toed boots turn their strut rooster and immortal,
the way Dan gave that little wave at the end of the show,
his rough hand fluttering, yes, like a bird
that has landed eternally on our waters.

TWO STANZAS ON MY FATHER BEGUN BY SHARON OLDS

Finally I gave up and became my father.
His third-son abasements; the scrimped-on hair.
I made everyone feel guilty about eating and further
kept a corner of the house so dirty no one could go there

without fear, while soapboxing about germs, about how clean
I am. I had drowned before you see, I had been
clunked on the head and now I would be lord or child, nothing in between.

*

You are always with me, a flowering
branch suspended over my life.
Since I was young, the flame of you raising,
lowering, edged every day with a light

not outside of dark: your familial duties, an essential routine
threaded through with puns, news, plots; your keen
sense of the world, you the rock on which all us water leaned.

THIS IS A PICTURE OF MY FATHER RIGHT AFTER I WAS BORN

This is a picture of my father
right after I was born.

His hair was dark then; his beard
a forest with the lake of his mouth in it,

grinning. Smiling so intensely, in fact,
that he had to hold his head in his hands

so it wouldn't fall apart from happiness
and his ignorance over what having me would mean.

I was just past blood then, swaddled,
and he in scrubs, and we met each other

first in that realm, I crying out and he
so young in all his confused love for me

and somewhere outside the frame my mother
was getting stitched up and the slow

song of her milk
was coming in.

POEMS THAT VEER INTO THE FREAKISH AND MAY ECHO JOHN ASHBERY

THE CONFIDANTE OF BRUISED FRUIT AND OTHER RIDES ON THE SUBWAY

Desperately solo this sunrise I find myself
talking to the photo of John Ashbery on the dust jacket
of his *Selected Later Poems*, addressing his stalwart,
bemused countenance (slightly askew Eton collar, the slim
rivulets of his silver hair) as if he were Christ, or the Buddha,
or just a gentle light bulb of a man.

Surely nothing in my life is less coherent than your poems,
I say, and yet they too have their incontrovertible charm.
In fact, I am addicted to their non-sequiturial beauty.

So why such sorrow over my own life's leaps and declivities,
John Ashbery? Should I not be celebrating the whole surreal
mess of it all? And in my hard solitude, I make the paper John
nod and respond with something entirely irrelevant and perfect
like "the oranges were grinning in the vineyard that April and
Mr Pompadour decided to doff his top hat."

2:22 A.M.

for Tomasz

I woke from a dream in which you had a wound on your head.
You can't stay awake in lectures otherwise.
It was not moist. It was not conditional.
Something was groomed about this injury and unlike the others
it did not go on for pages without saying anything.
A dark beer on the roughly hewn table, a faux-ethnic ambiance.
I remember the word *blue* and how you stumbled, loved
in the beautiful circles of poems, coached me in Spinoza
on how not to, effectively, deploy.
Yet the grey day accepted nothing, such predictable accumulations,
stratospheric, a disco of academe.
I forgot to mention the wound was opaque. Unlike you,
it evidenced closure.
Your notebook full of luminous erasures, intertextual
amorousness, the server's patterned dress torn a little
at the margins.
Maybe more than that.
How still we are silken, ravaged, as the moment we first met,
strutting in that field of tongues, piled high with signifiers.
Tick. Tick. Tick.
The clock has little red boots on, never apologizes.

LATER ON IN JANUARY, FOLLOWING THE CENTURY'S GRAND UPHEAVAL

So I realized Waldo is, in fact, a woman,
a tiny old lady in striped winter garments,
who I must find amid all the other fashionable imposters in Wonderland.

Yes, I would have liked to have attended the rally against
patriarchal underwear, but being around that many others all
chanting similar vocables gives me the sensation I'm a clone

and I can't overcome this feeling, even for clean water and universal daycare.
I fail that way. And in most others according to my best friend, Pepe,
who has established a seminar on the range of modes of saying you're sorry

and other hors d'oeuvres. Life is always shifting.
Sometimes you're a garbage picker in the House of Love and then, suddenly,
the divan is yours for the day, complete with silly slave boys gifting you whole

minutes of lusty fun. I don't know what to tell you anymore.
That I will be lying on the floor in dumb contemplation of stucco Rorschachs
or that I shall snap out of this miasma fast and return to being that wise

and eternally smiling adult. At any rate, the sky remains a kind
of sherbet colour. And some spring birds are accidentally singing.

HOOKS AND PULLEYS GALORE

Adulting is the new verb for when everything
starts to fall asunder in the flesh while the politics of the world
twinge more urgently and the bills still get paid.

O Mr. Joshua's taking down his decorations.
The *Merry*'s gone and now the *Happy*
too. Must be after Epiphany. (Over and over again, it looks like he's

waving at you but he's simply rubbing off the adhesive.)
The only transformation to celebrate though is the evening snow that,
in coating tree and parking lot equally, has said something profound

about beauty and its transience. Even the coyote skull
on the swimming pool roof sports a cold pelt and ah, to snag it on a
marlin hook and lodge its wildness in my heart's weird shrine.

A FEW DELIGHTFUL SOUND BITES FROM A DOWNTOWN TRAGEDY IN THREE PARTS

> But since I don't understand myself, only segments
> of myself that misunderstand each other, there's no
> reason for you to want to, no way you could
> even if we both wanted it.
> **JOHN ASHBERY**, "A Poem of Unrest"

1.
So I sit in my happy face socks being maudlin.
If there are still voodoo dolls in this age of Barbie Almost
Becomes President, someone bought one with my aging mug
on it and is plunging pins into its batting with glee.
"All I know is, it's Wednesday and I'm going to work," the harried
blonde barks into her phone at Starbucks. Knowledge: a severely

2.
abridged edition. Yes, I'm aware you don't love me. It's OK, says my mouth
while my psyche has issues with loneliness. Holding hands is gross; hold
hands with me in public! Multiple personalities of the somewhat-busted
heart, though few come as close to sorrow as Jerry the Boxer –
"I'm just an old dog," he admits, "but someone should cuddle me at night anyway."
Alright, listen. Every onesie in the universe won't

3.
make us whole again and when being spat on is "a compliment, girl" then there
will be fewer calls for *tables d'hôtes* and strolls on the parapet by moonlight.
Of course gender is my obsessive topic and how people deal with death.
Not much else but sex and flowers and your final instructions on a 3 × 5 lined
recipe card that you are sorry you haven't covered all costs, we can sing
the requiescat and you want the casket closed.

ELEGY WITH THE GHOST OF LARRY LEVIS IN IT

I used to like to say the names of corporations,

never knowing they had no feeling for me - Bendorf

Verster   Bernardin   Stong's -

they were sounds I couldn't understand and so they

stayed magic that whole century of childhood when

stone lions whispered and junks sailed in the stucco

of Helen's wall.

There are so many things I still don't want explained.

Like the Triumvirate of Nineveh or "'Twas brillig" or

why I wept for Sennacherib.

The exclusivity of the past can remain, a closed

land without clocks, an eternal animate instant, really.

*

So sail with me, silver river.

Every morning I worship this glitter and hold

the small corrupt tugs to my heart

as if I can't comprehend poison.

Some illusions – Nietzsche wrote –

the fish hooks of his opus shimmering

are in fact necessary, and not evidence

of the herd mentality but about keeping

antimonies alive.

I'm paraphrasing the day, of course

and the breadth of his desire as he waited

for Salome's whip to lick his flesh pure and dirty.

*

There is no elegy without death.

We know this.

Right?

But our era's anonymous poet, that tenth-grade

hacker of NASA, may beg to differ, slipping

into another universe entirely, yodelling

"Death, be not proud" from the technological

Pyrenees where the beginning of the long dash

is not followed by ten seconds of silence

and the untested Emergency Broadcast System

but is only a hobo now as Norma from Jeanne Mance

still calls them, perhaps warming its dot matrix

paws above a polyethylene glycol fire.

I know I don't want to die on Mars.

There is little else I can be sure of.

THE SOCIAL NET AS STURM UND DRANG

The ad infinitum unreeling of stuff and stuff
and stuff, everyday dreck of John does this and
Jenny does that, how much must you attend it?

You must nothing in fact, but breathe in and out
like a sexed machine and make sure the cats
have *agua*, the heliotrope, light. Sure a few

shekels may be required to sustain your pizza
habit, your hunger for composing poems, but
simplify, suck out the cellulite in your methods,

go undercover as yourself. Told many times
there is only this moment, embossing memes
of it on every virtual wall with rainbows and

posies will not, in itself, make you stop to sniff
the delirium. Cut out the cant, the rot of yah
and yar and is anybody out there, please, I just

posted a photo of my loneliness?
Be alone in feline composure, think thoughts
wrapt in fur, doze elongated or splayed,

quell the torture of must and should.
There, I have given you your mantras,
I frenetically scribbling this opus to absolve

everything, "Sanctus Mundi," Modus Vivendi,
"Buongiorno Tristezza," Hallelujah, again.

TRANSFORMATIONS IN THE AVIARY OF THE BANAL

O pigeons, you will never be mystical –
you have not learned to incorporate bookmarks
so from the pages of the *Best American Poetry*
a pamphlet called *How to Survive a D & C*
flutters out, while on the mantelpiece is displayed
your womb, bronzed and final as baby shoes.

O gulls, you will never predict the future –
does using allspice versus nutmeg truly matter
you think and thus though your lexicon is accurate
your meals fall into abstraction and you end up
applying for a grant to study the attenuated claws
of your cat as evidence for more proximate constellations.

O starlings, you will never be fashionable –
eros being bound to the ineffable and I
have made the mistake of sporting white and perhaps
also blue eyeshadow back when I was but a mere apple
trembling on the tree of adolescence yet since then
I have become a pataphysicist beneath a holy feathered mobile

Of words.

EXCERPTS FROM THE DIARY OF JOHANN HAUSER'S WOMAN (1985)

Maria Gugging Psychiatric Clinic

January 14, 1986

    Today, I played the piano with my breasts. Why not?
    They are like torpedoes, like the bosom of God.
    I played Chopin and the crazy man turned the pages for me.
    We tried to play a duet but my hips are too big.
    They curve out in layers like onion skins.
    They echo like the sounds of a bell.
    Just as we began the "Revolutionary Étude," he lost
    his balance on the stool and down he went to the floor.
    I had to play the rest from memory while he lay
    there like a worm.
    My breasts became bruised with all that fortissimo.

March 26, 1989

    My mother used to say I have the face of the *Pietà*.
    I do not know whether she meant gracious
    or long-suffering.

March 27, 1989

    The problem, when it comes down to it, is the structure
    of it all. A body that bleeds out of the margins of the Bible
    and is still expected to be holy.
    My vagina is an old pear.
    Pears have always been, from the beginning of time,
    heathen.

October 5, 1990

> For years, they tied me up. For my own good, of course.
> I had been trying to climb inside my navel, to be reborn
> in the dark plum of my womb.
> Boredom makes me inventive.
> I had cross-stitched and painted and square danced
> enough.

November 13, 1991

> The crazy man visited me today. He shouldn't be in my room.
> He'd heard my rays calling out to his rays.
> Sometimes this happens. He kissed the top of my tiny head
> and my large red body quivered.
> That's all I can say about it.
> Dinner was served.
> And the pills came around again.

JUST ANOTHER TYPICAL DAY

Just another typical day on the SkyTrain. The kraken
chasing me about, trying to spit on my Versace mind, the chest
I've crafted in dreams of Barbie's sweet ride, my old child face.

What can I say about us anymore other than that no, we will never be joining
the Rosary of the Month Club.
Suburbia is only slightly bereft.

The cemetery empties itself gradually, transfers its shrinking humans
into smaller and smaller boxes, each complete with iPhone pockets
for every grain of ash.

While I keep writing these poems only encryptable in Aphrodite's papyrus
and nothing I create will bring you back, draw you closer or otherwise
replace the batteries on this Energizer reptile of a heart.

THE ARCHAIC BODY

was not redeemable in nip-and-tuck afternoons, collagen cocktails,
silicone confections but sagged with the gravity of the cave, or
held in stays, had only its allotted
moment

did not spend "life as a module" but existence as a baby hutch,
braying kin forth to perish of coughs, lead poisoning,
a sabre-toothed
pinnacle

could not cement its identity with Kodak's instant but with lineage,
stone's echoes, oil daubing all the children named
John, stick figures stark,
undifferentiated

knew what it was to starve, to sink in a constellation of smallpox from eligible
to old maid, to be toothless, blind at twelve or crooked
by rickets into circus-shape, fate-
marred

held its own in the marriage market, be-noosed for a pen'orth, trumped
by hucksters hungry for dowries (coach and four, five grand a year),
being dragged by the hair little
better

saw its end in debtor's prison, the last hunt's rictus, a hemorrhage of dirty
hands, the scaffold where it was disembowelled or merely
burned in order that modesty be
preserved

revelled that it was an afterlife, halfway to rising at the right-hand side
of the deity in his day of judgment when the flesh that kept his temple
would be whole,
renewed

was formed from a homunculus, took its lineaments in the flayed
light of a male cadaver, posed for Rembrandt, rode androgynous into
the sunset. In an eighteenth-century
almanac,

the archaic body is shown to possess two parts no longer living among us:
an arrow pointing to the groin contains the word *secrets*,
an arrow to the heart holds

reins

A BRIEF HISTORY OF GETTING NAKED

In the beginning, all was buggery, pederasty
and the missionary position, Hellenic teens

twisting to the call, "Hey, boys, turn around,"
a Leiden coin depicting the penetrating stare

of penetration, some maids relishing the anomaly
of Ovid's verse in which the nipples and thighs

> were as much a part of lust as the face, their darkly
> carved genitalia. Two thousand years before such a chronicle

> of eroticism recommences, the prudish stretch of silence
> yawing outside the ever-horny courts as nighttime

> mounting predominates – "no kissing, please, we're British" –
> sex solely for the keyhole of anus or cunt, flouting

the bugaboo of procreation or doing the king's
duty, either way the thought of exchanging saliva,

choking down ejaculate or even embracing at length
in the roseate light of a boudoir nixed by the spectre

of scabies, lice, forcing Casanova to curtail his libertinism
to itch, and then there was death. Fifty per cent of women expiring

> in childbirth, corpses laid out in the parlour, sombre dicta
> against frivolity, not to mention granny squinting over her tatting

> by the fire, ready to haul out the donkey on which desirous
> women were trotted while being socked with Guernsey oranges.

> Between smallpox and the failure rate of French letters, few
> lascivious wenches were found, eager to flash the pink

to strangers, romp in Elysian fields of flesh. Not until the late
nineteenth century did the incandescent body surface, less deathly,

less clad, frolicking in post-Romantic nature, tupped
off its pedestal, champagne-fizzed and Bacchic-nymphed,

Dos Passos, Valentine de Saint-Point, Colette rising towards
the honed Sandow of muscle and outdoors vigour, ladies

    straddling bicycles, men sportive. After the wars,
    steeped in the heat of *Chatterley*, Kinsey's throbbing data,

    sex bubbles up as a middle-class pastime, Betty Crocker
    fellating Mr. Clean on the kitchen table, Enovid opening

    the '60s to a release from unwanted Juniors, women everywhere
    strutting Quant and leafing through *Cosmo*, kneeling to

cunnilingus as a heated political platform while gay men
melted notions of perversity in the anonymity of bathhouses.

Little Richard crowed over having his male nipples sucked;
Sutcliffe's padlocks became *de rigueur* for suburban

dominatrixes as they flogged passivity to sleep, the shift
complete and the body laid bare, surmounting disease,

    archaic laws, flaunting its butches, femmes, its fairies,
    unleashing deviancies at once-Tupperware parties,

    parading the hedonic, not on the shaming back of a mule,
    but from the colourful Roman floats that roll each summer

    down Robson Street, hordes flaunting boas and ginches,
    Martial's ghost stirring in their rainbows.

CONEY ISLAND, OCTOBER 2008

The Shoot the Freak neon zizzes
        and sparks, slung in its weary marquee

between a poisonous night café
        and the boarded-up jazz of ball tosses,

pricey fried oysters. The sanitation workers are bored;
        slump by the privy with plastic

bags of buns and all the leftover summer gulls.
        A man hawks Obama condoms on the swept

lengths of the boardwalk where spires of bamboo bob
        past the metal palm tree, commemorating Sukkot.

Ah ya shoulda been here two months ago when it was
        cotton floss and onion cakes, the last vendor

of the season cries out, but for us there are
        no glory days, just the Wonder Wheel's

hush, the shushing of the saltless ocean beyond
        the ghost of Madame Twisto –

her beautiful, convoluting limbs.

FREAKS

On the subway over the Hudson, an armless man puffs
       into the harmonica slotted into its yoke
around his neck and, pitying his lack of prosthetics,

passengers drop pennies in his Starbucks cup, stare
       out the graffitied glass at the black
wake behind him. There is no longer any fanfare

for his strangeness, his Darwinian
       predicament. Once Barnum and his freaks
took to the rails, a herd of wonders clacking from Mississauga

to Minneapolis, fats, dwarfs, giants, tribes, Jo-Jo
       the Dog-Faced Boy, Admiral Dot the midget, Jane
de Vere whose 14-inch beard flowed darkly over her corset, three

rings of lymphedemal limbs, double vaginas and ectrodactylic
       hands, posing in Eisenmann's faux parlours on the Bowery,
wearing real furs, taking tea with Queen Victoria, whose boudoir

flaunted its own pickled punk amid snuff and fans.
       We have laser machines, wax and scalpels so that
smooth, proportioned, we can attain to the level of technicians,

programmers, torn from the noble pantheon of curiosities,
       birthed into the invisible world of acceptance.
Why didn't they let me live in another century, stay

bird woman, alligator girl, with my extra set of molars, that
       one incisor that stuck out from my palate, waiting
for its untenable shell. How I would have boxed with Zip

the Pinhead, quaffed one back with Lobster Man, lolled about
 with Corpulent Blanche, then every night the gilded
applause as I parade in my cage, sweet princess of feathers,

 while now, extracted, braced, perfected, I am lonely.

JOHN ASHBERY, I WANT YOU TO KEEP WHISPERING YOUR SWEET NOTHINGS IN MY EAR FOREVER OR A VALENTINE'S DAY POEM TO POETRY

If I could choose anyone to wake to it would be you,
old gay perpetrator of textual divagations.
I never know where you're going to go next and that's
fine by me, the girl who has learned to live with circuses,
and bits of bread and dead men and a womb full of hairballs spat up
by wrong turns on the friendly genetic highway.
You reassure me with your floating prepositions and
paratactic wanderings that it's mostly joyous so little is fixed
or at least that the melancholia has melody in it, if the foot tapping
often veers into Tourette's and then back again to a nostalgic
school dance in the autochthonous Hebrides.
O John Ashbery, you are what I resisted as a younger
poet but who now, I embrace (of course, platonically).
You make the melee OK and the mayhem
just another wild day at Sobeys.
And so I won't rouse you from your dreaming, but if you
should stir past noon, please note the tiniest grapefruit I
placed on the bedside table, how
it winks its juices at you like the most eligible bachelor on Mars.

IF ELIOT WERE TO WRITE YOUR PERSONAL APOCALYPSE

No, this is the way the world ends:
we are dying and someone texts us furniture,
a kind of wood-and-tile band-aid against ashes.
Your inbox has many offers of riches from
the Emperor of Bahrain and every time
you go online your brain, fissured by a million splinters, repeats
I'm OK and I don't care if you're OK, too.
We have no true metaphors for the poetic anymore,
but that old hunger won't abate,
so instead we turn it into an industry
and in this way receive a dinette set, at least.
At least there is this.
You are dying in a renovated room, well appointed and clean.
The dream has been fulfilled,
perhaps you will even be able to afford to maintain
your post-mortem web page, which flashes image after image of you, a corpse
in your castle of things whimpering, I love you, I love you, Sandra Dee.
Yes, how you wanted to believe in the furniture and the whimpering.

ACKNOWLEDGEMENTS

Some of the poems found in this collection were originally published in the following literary journals and anthologies:

"Residual Lingerie" in *Connotation Press: An Online Artifact* (US)

"The Window Washer" in *The Antigonish Review*

"Swallows' Nests of Isla de Janitzio, Michoacán" in *New Plains Review* (US)

"Just Another Loss of Faith" in *Connotation Press: An Online Artifact* (US)

"The Combination" in *The Conium Review* (US)

"My Parents are Playing Scrabble on the Deck" in *Connotation Press: An Online Artifact* (US)

"2:22 a.m." in *Prick of the Spindle* (US)

"Elegy with the Ghost of Larry Levis in It" in *Luna Luna Magazine* (US)

"Excerpts from the Diary of Johann Hauser's *Woman* (1985)" in *PAPER Magazine* (US); *Borderline* (US); *Force Field: 77 Women Poets of British Columbia* (Mother Tongue, 2013)

"The Archaic Body" in *The Malahat Review*

"A Brief History of Getting Naked" in *Precipice*

"Coney Island, October 2008" in *PRISM international* (Runner-up for the Earle Birney Prize)

"Freaks" in *Splash of Red* (US); *Do Not Look at the Sun* (France); *Force Field: 77 Women Poets of British Columbia* (Mother Tongue, 2013)

"If Eliot Were to Write Your Personal Apocalypse" in *Arc Poetry Magazine*

NOTES

The film world is full of lingo. For these poems you may need to know a few terms.

gak: set things up or dress a set. Can be used as a noun or verb. Gack, however, is an expression of disgust.

three-holer: a moveable washroom, while the honey wagon is a loo attached to the AD's trailer.

Crafty: craft services, where the goodies are. They also serve sandwiches and hot snack each shift.

BGs: background actors or extras.

circus: where the star trailers and production vehicles are located.

Abby shot: the second to last shot of the day.

duves: short for *duvateens* or black fabric pieces usually used by grips.

Blonde, Long Arm, the Shotgun, the Chimera and atomics (along with gels, flaps, tabs): some equipment an electric uses to light the set, basically speaking.

copy: I heard you and I'm doing it.

pretties: what the hair/makeup department used to be called.

Window: last shot of the day, also known as the martini.

CATHERINE OWEN is the author of ten collections of poetry and three of prose, including her compilation of interviews on writing called *The Other 23 & a Half Hours: Or Everything You Wanted to Know that Your MFA Didn't Teach You* (Wolsak & Wynn, 2015) and her short story collection, *The Day of the Dead* (Caitlin Press, 2016). Her work has been nominated for awards, toured Canada eight times, and appeared in anthologies, as well as translations. She has been employed by both the Locations and the Props department in TV land, plays metal bass and has two cats: Solstice and Equinox.